# In Passing

*poems by*

# Deborah Cooper

*Finishing Line Press*
Georgetown, Kentucky

# In Passing

Copyright © 2021 by Deborah Gordon Cooper
ISBN 978-1-64662-467-6 First Edition
All rights reserved under International and Pan-American Copyright Conventions.
No part of this book may be reproduced in any manner whatsoever without written permission from the publisher, except in the case of brief quotations embodied in critical articles and reviews.

Publisher: Leah Huete de Maines

Editor: Christen Kincaid

Cover Art: Joel Cooper

Author Photo: Joel Cooper

Cover Design: Elizabeth Maines McCleavy

Printed in the USA on acid-free paper.
Order online: www.finishinglinepress.com
        also available on amazon.com

Author inquiries and mail orders:
Finishing Line Press
P. O. Box 1626
Georgetown, Kentucky 40324
U. S. A.

# Table of Contents

Invitation ................................................................... 1

Watching the Waves ................................................ 3

Morning Star ............................................................ 4

Lost and Found ........................................................ 5

You Will Find Me ................................................... 7

Tulips ........................................................................ 8

Small Boy ................................................................. 9

Hollander Road ...................................................... 10

Becoming ................................................................ 11

In Passing ............................................................... 13

Untethering ............................................................ 15

*for my brothers,
the Gordon boys*

*Gregory, Roderick,
Cameron, Jonathan
& Drew*

**Invitation**

Walk out each day
in every temperament
of weather
and choose one thing
to save.

Set it in the blue bowl
of the heart
or add it to the page

be it a hawk,
a frosted branch,
a passing face…
traces of warmth there
or of wanting.

Listen deeply
be it a meadowlark, a creek
or someone's sorrow.

Make of your listening
an open field
where windblown seeds
take hold.

Make of your listening
a garden.

Forgive someone.

Notice how a tiny cage
swings open
deep inside you
and a bird flies free.

Always sleep beside
an open window;
never draw the drapes
or shut the shade

so that the moonlight
and the owl's shadow
sweep the bed.

Keep the window open
in all seasons,
even in the winter
just a crack

so that, while you sleep
you breathe the night

filling your body
with a million stars.

**Watching the Waves**

if you can wait
enough

if you can stay
a little longer
than you'd planned

if you have practiced
being still
and empty

letting go of your words
to make a space
in you

you might say blue
or silver

you might say shimmering
or thundering
or drum

or evanescence
or eternity.

When you are still at last

when you are wordless,
waiting

you might feel
the waters breathe

a breath that enters you

as easily
as light might fill
even the darkest hollow.

**Morning Star**

Mary was her childhood's
favorite god

the endless litany of names

mother of mercy,
morning star,
wellspring of peace.

Her brothers,
in their cassocks
and their surplices

assured her
*real gods must be boys*

but she ignored them

adorned in rosary beads

humming a hymn
of her own.

**Lost and Found**

She lost her first faith
somewhere in the pew,
between the pages
of commandments

between the souls
of the redeemed
and all the others
with no hope
of getting in.

She lost her first faith
somewhere in the pew,
and found another
in the April yard

the polished curls
of almost-leaves
along a bending branch

the scent of earth and rain
and purple in the air.

She lost her first faith
somewhere in the pew

and found another
in whatever took her hand

unlatched the gate
for any stray or wanderer

the one eyed dog,
the scrawny, matted cat

the fallen robin's egg
that she would tend for weeks

keep in a nest of socks
beneath her bed,
and sing to in the night

the quiet hymn
about the morning
and the first bird.

**You Will Find Me**

Somewhere
between the budding
and the blossom

in the song
between the blossom
and the bee

between the tree
and its reflection.

Between the lake
and the coral clouds
of morning

between the forest
and the starlings'
reverie

between the landscape
and the longing

between the music
and the music's
memory.

**Tulips**

All day, she carries
the tulips he sent

in lieu of a visit

from room to room,
following the sun

to coax the blossoms,
folded in their buds.

She sees the petals
pressing at the seams

the way that hope
swells in the throat

the way it angles
for the light

the hope that chose
the biscuits
that he favors

and the honey
for his tea.

She sleeps
with the flowers
on her nightstand.

In the dark
she hears the tulips
breathe.

**Small Boy**

This morning
she opens her eyes

and it is snowing again
or maybe still

outside the window.

She shuts her eyes again

not because she minds
the snow

but to find her way
into the dream
again

to take the small hand
of the small boy
in hers

a braid of blood
and bone

of memory
and skin

enough to hold him

but the window's closed

the path, blown over.

## Hollander Road

The swayback barn
has fallen in upon itself

the farmhouse, gone

a few scattered stones
from the hearth

she pockets one,
tosses another

finds a doorknob
in the overgrown weeds

the baby's room,
she knows

for the memory
it wakens in her palm

she takes this too,
though she scarcely needs a charm

for wherever she might find herself

the winds
across these fields
blow through her still

the sigh of cottonwoods

and there, inside of her

three white horses
in the early morning fog

disappearing
and appearing.

**Becoming**

The fragile hand
of the woman in the pew

rests on her husband's
trembling arm

his rounded shoulder,
narrow back

the ring on her finger
catching the light.

Green lingers
in the trees

as if the leaves
are reluctant
to turn

but hover
on the cusp

of peach or rose,
of rust or scarlet

a pause of breath
between the known
and the next

a hesitation,
then the swimmer
diving in

becomes the water

we are becoming
and becoming.

Green lingers
in the trees

as if the leaves
are reluctant
to turn.

The calling
of the loons
across the bay

echoes inside of us

echoes inside.

## In Passing

1

The smell of burning leaves
makes her feel everything
at once

takes her beyond
the slender confines
of her body.

2

Stars cluster
in a corner
of the window

she lights a candle
on the sill

a constellation falls.

3

In dreams

her lifted hands
are scarlet blossoms

opening
and unfolding

like a prophecy.

4

Dark clouds this morning,
casting shadows
on the waves

and still,
the birds sing

one of sorrow,
two of grace.


5

The sound of a piano
through an open window

carried by the wind

turns her own taut spine
to a plucked string.


6

The sea of scent
released by
one blue hyacinth

and she believes again.

## Untethering

She imagines
she can live
in one sparse room

a slender bed,
a single chair
beside a window.

But by bit
she gives her past away

the china teacups
rung with strands
of tiny violets

the rosary,
the ring

as if she is unfastening
her history

one button at a time.

The old poems
make a beautiful fire.

She writes a new one
by its light.

She writes
the window open
to the moon.

She writes the dunes.
She writes the sea.

Deborah Cooper is the author of six collections of poetry, including *Between the Ceiling & the Moon* (Finishing Line Press 2008), *Under the Influence of Lilacs* (Clover Valley Press 2010) and *Blue Window* (Clover Valley Press 2017). Deborah's work has been published in numerous journals and anthologies, among them two collections by her writing group of over thirty years, most recently *Bound Together: Like the Grasses* (Clover Valley Press 2013). She has co-edited three anthologies published by Holy Cow Press. (*Beloved on the Earth, The Heart of All That Is,* and *Amethyst & Agate*)

Deborah and her husband, Joel, a printmaker, often work in tandem and frequently exhibit their shared images. She has worked with visual artists, musicians, dancers and theater groups.

Deborah has conducted writing circles with homeless individuals in her community. She has taught poetry classes in jails and juvenile centers for many years. Deborah was honored to serve as the Duluth Minnesota Poet Laureate from 2012 to 2014.

www.ingramcontent.com/pod-product-compliance
Lightning Source LLC
LaVergne TN
LVHW041526070426
835507LV00013B/1844